I0089532

MATTHEW RYAN's work includes: *Kelly* (Queensland Theatre Company 2012), *boy girl wall* co-written with Lucas Stibbard (The Escapists/Melbourne Theatre Company 2012/Critical Stages National Australian Tour 2012/La Boite Theatre Company 2011/Hothouse Theatre 2011/Adelaide Fringe 2010/Metro Arts 2010/2009), *The Harbinger* co-written with David Morton (Dead Puppet Society/La Boite Theatre Company 2012), *French Twist* (Queensland Theatre Company 2011 as 'Sacre Bleu'), *Attack Of The Attacking Attackers!* (The Escapists/La Boite Theatre Company 2008), *Summer Wonderland* (La Boite Theatre Company 2007), *Chasing The Whale* (La Boite Theatre Company 2005/ATYP 2000 as 'The Dance of Jeremiah') and *So You Die A Little* co-written with Tony Brockman (Pandemonium Theatre 1998).

Matthew has developed a series of works for young performers through Backbone Youth Arts called *Plays From The Top Of The Stairs*.

Matthew received the Queensland Theatre Company's George Landen Dann award for *Chasing The Whale* (as 'The Dance of Jeremiah') in 2000, the Matilda Award for Best New Australian Work for *Attack Of The Attacking Attackers!* in 2008 and the Matilda Award for Best Independent Production in 2011 for *boy girl wall*.

Matthew is a co-founder of the award winning theatre-making group The Escapists.

Leon Cain as Dan and Steven Rooke as Ned in the 2012 Queensland Theatre Company production. (Photo: Rob MacColl.)

KELLY

Matthew Ryan

CURRENCY PRESS

CURRENCY PLAYS

First published in 2013
by Currency Press Pty Ltd,
PO Box 2287, Strawberry Hills, NSW, 2012, Australia
enquiries@currency.com.au
www.currency.com.au

Kelly copyright © Matthew Ryan, 2013

COPYING FOR EDUCATIONAL PURPOSES
The Australian *Copyright Act* 1968 (Act) allows a maximum of one chapter or 10% of this book, whichever is the greater, to be copied by any educational institution for its educational purposes provided that that educational institution (or the body that administers it) has given a remuneration notice to Copyright Agency Limited (CAL) under the Act. For details of the CAL licence for educational institutions contact CAL, Level 15, 233 Castlereagh Street, Sydney, NSW, 2000. Tel: within Australia 1800 066 844 toll free; outside Australia +61 2 9394 7600; Fax: +61 2 9394 7601; Email: info@copyright.com.au

COPYING FOR OTHER PURPOSES
Except as permitted under the Act, for example a fair dealing for the purposes of study, research, criticism or review, no part of this book may be reproduced, stored in a retrieval system, or transmitted in any form or by any means without prior written permission. All enquiries should be made to the publisher at the address above.

Any performance or public reading of *Kelly* is forbidden unless a licence has been received from the author or the author's agent. The purchase of this book in no way gives the purchaser the right to perform the play in public, whether by means of a staged production or a reading. All applications for public performance should be addressed to Kubler Auckland Management, PO Box 1062, Milton, QLD, 4064. Tel: +61 7 3368 1700; Email: brisbane@ kublerauckland.com.

The moral right of the author has been asserted.

NATIONAL LIBRARY OF AUSTRALIA CIP DATA

Author:	Ryan, Matthew, 1978– author.
Title:	Kelly / Matthew Ryan.
ISBN:	9780868199870 (paperback)
Subjects:	Kelly, Ned, 1855–1880.
	Bushrangers—Australia—Drama.
Dewey Number:	A822.4.

Typeset by Claire Grady for Currency Press.
Front cover shows Steven Rooke as Ned in the 2012 Queensland Theatre Company production
(Photo: Rob MacColl).
Cover design by Katy Wall for Currency Press.

Currency Press acknowledges the Traditional Owners of the Country on which we live and work. We pay our respects to all Aboriginal and Torres Strait Islander Elders, past and present.

Kelly was created with assistance from the Commonwealth Government through the Australia Council, its arts funding and advisory body.

Contents

Writer's Note

The first 'Kelly Play' took place the day Ned died, with his traumatised sister Kate paid to sit in a chair while hundreds of people paraded past staring at her. She did it to pay the legal costs of trying to free her mother from prison. Those efforts failed. And years later, Kate drowned herself.

Kelly Plays were all the rage for the next sixty years. Huge money-makers, they ranged from dramatic onstage shoot-outs to horse stunt shows to the world's first feature film. By the 1940s, there was barely a theatre in the country that didn't have a Ned Kelly helmet tucked away in the costume room. Retold again and again, the story became a cultural myth. Facts blurred with fiction. And Ned was always the hero.

Modern Australian Theatre has been silent on Ned Kelly. His story was considered old and dusty, relegated to awkward historical recreations and Victorian tourist attractions. The myth of the hero had drowned out the more complex story of the man himself.

I spent a few years of my childhood living in 'Kelly Country' in rural Victoria. There was no question to the people in that area: Ned was a hero. Simple as that. Yet, even as a kid, I wasn't convinced. I have remained fascinated by the figure of Ned ever since, that defiant towering Australian who apparently epitomised the Australian spirit, when every action he took seemed in contrast to our laid-back, non-confrontational national character.

After moving to sunny Brisbane, I discovered the myth of Dan Kelly—that he survived the Siege of Glenrowan and ran away to Queensland under another name, erasing the past for a calmer present. It doesn't get more Queensland than that.

A story took over my mind, a confrontation between two titans of our history. I wanted to breathe new life into the Kelly story. I wanted to smash the myth and the true story against each other. Ned as assured defiant history, Dan as the uncertain present. Complete opposites of each other, even their names (almost).

More importantly, I wanted it to be real. An event. An argument you might hear at the back of a pub and move away from in fear of danger.

I wanted real anger and real humour. And if I couldn't give them guns, I was going to give them lines that rang out like gunshots.

Sometimes, while writing this play in the middle of the night, I felt ghosts nearby. Men standing among the trees outside, keeping watch. I've never felt it before and I doubt I'll ever feel it again. The spirits of men, making sure.

So here it is. My Kelly Play.

Minus the helmet.

Acknowledgements

A huge thank you to Wesley Enoch, Todd MacDonald and everyone at Queensland Theatre Company. To the amazing cast and crew of the production. To everyone who helped me along the way. To Shari Irwin for her love, support and feedback (and for convincing me the original title was crap). To my family for moving to Victoria where the first spark was lit.

And to the ghosts outside—I hope they are satisfied.

Kelly was first produced by Queensland Theatre Company at Cremorne Theatre, Brisbane, on 15 September 2012, with the following cast:

NED KELLY	Steven Rooke
DAN KELLY	Leon Cain
GUARD	Hugh Parker

Director, Todd MacDonald
Designer, Simone Romaniuk
Lighting Designer, Ben Hughes
Composer / Sound Designer, Guy Webster
Stage Manager, Peter Sutherland
Assistant Stage Manager, Shaun O'Rourke
Fight Director, Niki-J Price

The role of the GUARD was later played by Anthony Standish.

CHARACTERS

NED KELLY
DAN KELLY
GUARD
KENNEDY, JIM, STEELE

The actor who plays the guard plays all other roles.

SETTING

The play takes place in a gaol cell.

NED KELLY *in his gaol cell, hands cuffed and chained together.*

A GUARD *enters.*

NED: Fuck, you're an ugly bastard.

GUARD: You have a visitor.

NED: Not in a general sense either. It's a very specific lack of appeal you suffer from. It's your eyes. You have pig's eyes. Has anyone ever told you that? They're bastards if they haven't. Man deserves to know if he resembles a pig. How are you supposed to know? Can't look at yourself. Not with any objectivity on the matter.

GUARD: Do you want your visitor or not?

NED: Who is it?

GUARD: A priest.

NED: Christ. Are there any left in the whole of Melbourne?

GUARD: This one says he knows you.

NED: Haven't they all said the same thing?

GUARD: I'll tell him no then?

NED: Did you give them my letter?

GUARD: Yes. I did.

NED: And?

GUARD: And they agreed. Said fair was fair.

NED: My mother?

GUARD: Released.

NED: She's free?

GUARD: Staying with your family. In some big fancy hotel.

NED: My funeral?

GUARD: Agreed to that to.

NED: A cemetery? Consecrated ground I asked for.

GUARD: Oh, yes. Headstone. Whole works.

NED: Right. Right then.

      NED *laughs to himself, satisfied.*

GUARD: Kelly. I'm lying. [*Laughing*] They're not letting that mad bitch out of gaol.

NED *advances on the* GUARD. *The* GUARD *draws his truncheon.*

NED *stops.*

You go right ahead, Kelly. You just keep walking straight towards me.

NED: Would you do well, I wonder? Better than the other ones at least? Because they didn't do very well at all.

GUARD: Heard they picked a nice spot for your body. Out in the yard. Where the boys take their shit. Heard they want to bury you with your mouth open. Face up, nice and grateful like, for when it makes its way down to you.

NED: Is that right?

GUARD: Yeah, that's right.

NED: Well, at least I'm handsome. Unlike yourself, who's so ugly the loneliest dog in the world wouldn't fuck your face.

The GUARD *laughs.* NED *joins him.*

GUARD: That's pretty funny.

NED: Thank you.

GUARD: Wonder if you'll be so funny tomorrow. Can't wait to see it myself. Got a nice little spot all picked out.

NED: Tell me where and I'll give you a little wave. That'll be me being funny.

GUARD: Be hard to see me. Quite the crowd coming apparently.

NED: Well, I am very well known.

GUARD: They're coming to see you get what you deserve.

NED: Deserve? Read the newspaper. I'm a national fucking hero.

GUARD: I thought heroes got medals.

NED: It's a matter of great contention.

GUARD: What about Fitzpatrick? You a hero to him? The man you shot in your own home? Or Stringybark Creek? Coppers you killed in cold blood?

NED: Don't recall my blood being all that cold.

GUARD: What about Glenrowan? A few died there. Your whole gang if I recall. Your own brother. Burnt to a crisp, wasn't he? You a hero to him?

NED *takes out a scrap of newspaper and reads from it.*

NED: [*reading*] '…The grandest of all Australian fellows, destined to be nothing less than the father of our national character.' Do you have a newspaper article about yourself?

GUARD: Can't say I have.

NED: Ah.

GUARD: Been to my share of hangings though. You know what most of them say just before they drop? 'I'm sorry.' 'I'm sorry!' Piss themselves too, some of them. Know why? 'Cause they understand. In the end. That they deserve what's coming to them. When they pull that hood over your eyes? When you're staring at the black? You will too.

NED: Well now. That was borderline eloquent.

GUARD: I heard a rumour you had an army at Glenrowan. You heard that one? Supporters hiding in the trees, ready to attack. But when it came time to charge they were nowhere to be seen. Left you all to die. Doesn't sound like you were a very big hero to them.

NED: Are you after some form of physical conflict? Something to brag about to your mates down at the pub perhaps? I'm sure you'd be famous for it. Albeit a shit-shovel uglier than you are right now.

>   *Beat.*

GUARD: What do I tell your priest?

NED: Tell him I question the existence of a God that allows the innocent to suffer while the fat, wart-covered rich piglets who suckle at the teat of the heaving shit-covered England continue to run free.

GUARD: Christ.

NED: Don't blame him. He didn't make you an ugly bastard. Your mother squeezed too hard is all.

>   *The* GUARD *exits.*

>   [*Singing*] 'There's a land that is fairer than day.
>   And by faith we can see it afar;
>   For the Father waits over the way,
>   To prepare us a dwelling place there.
>   In the sweet by and by,
>   we shall meet on that beautiful shore.
>   In the sweet by and by,
>   we shall meet on that beautiful shore.'

DAN KELLY *enters dressed as a Priest, holding a bible, nervous.*

[*Calling off*] Did you not infer a no, you witless prick?

DAN *watches* NED. NED *doesn't look at* DAN.

DAN: Hello, Ned.

NED: Hello.

DAN: How are you?

NED: Oh. I'm fine, thank you. Yourself?

DAN: Fine.

NED: Good. Well, that covers everyone then.

DAN: Ned.

NED: I've been trying to think of some clever last words, Father. Something for people to remember me by. Do you have any suggestions?

DAN: No.

NED: I think it's important. Remembering. Would you agree, Father?

DAN: Depends on the man being remembered, I suppose.

NED: Jesus. What were his last words? I've been trying to recall.

DAN: He said 'Oh God, why have you forsaken me?'

NED: Christ, that's a bit rubbish.

DAN: He was dying at the time.

NED: Still. Give it a go.

DAN: Ned.

NED: Joe Byrne got a good one in. Held his glass high. 'To the Kelly Gang.' Bullets went straight through him. Poor bastard didn't even get his drink down.

DAN: Ned.

NED *looks at* DAN. *And recognises him.*

NED *lurches violently towards* DAN. DAN *steps back, scared.* NED *stops, glaring at him. They stare at each other.*

NED: Hello, Dan.

DAN: Hello, Ned.

NED: Not dead then?

DAN: No.

NED: That's a rather large fucking surprise, Dan.

DAN: I suppose it would be.

NED: The coppers set that place on fire. They burnt you to the ground.

DAN: I know.

NED: Your sisters held what was left of you and screamed their lungs out, handfuls of burnt meat coming off you. Who was it they were screaming for?

DAN: One of the hostages. He was dead. I threw my armour on him and got away through the smoke.

NED: Steve?

DAN: He's dead.

NED: Does Ma know?

DAN: No.

NED: Katie?

DAN: No one.

NED: You've not told your own family you're alive?

DAN: I thought it best to keep trouble away from them.

NED: You don't think they should know?

DAN: Not with the whole country watching them. [*Beat.*] Are you not glad to see me, Ned?

NED: Why would I not be glad to see you, Dan?

DAN: Because I got away. And you…

NED: And I what?

DAN: Got caught.

NED: Is that what happened? I recall a few more details than that. I recall a veritable fucking slew of them. [*Beat.*] So you won't see your own family but you come all the way to Melbourne Gaol? Through crowds and coppers. And into the lion's den.

DAN: Coppers don't look for dead men. Not that I wasn't pissing myself every step of the way.

NED: Costume and all. Must be wanting something pretty badly.

DAN: I came to say goodbye.

NED: Goodbye.

    Beat.

DAN: I came because of how things were left. Any misunderstandings you might have about the last time we saw each other.

NED: Yes. That was unusual.

DAN: I'm here to set it right. To part ways on good terms, as it were.

NED: And you must be desperate for it. To set foot in a room with me.

DAN: I'm leaving, Ned. Heading north. To Queensland.

NED: Queensland? Christ, I thought I was in for it.

DAN: I can work the sugar cane. It's summer all year up there. Like heaven, they reckon.

NED: Like heaven. And when are you coming back?

DAN: I won't be coming back. I'm going for good. They say you can forget yourself in Queensland. That it has no memory. Forget the past. Forget everything. New life. New name. The whole lot.

NED: You have a name.

DAN: I can't live with that name.

NED: And what about your family? Your mother in gaol, your sisters that need taking care of?

DAN: I can't live with that name.

NED: And what name will you have?

DAN: I haven't decided.

NED: Will it be a man's name?

DAN: I think that would suit.

NED: Do you? [*Beat*.] Do you know what the last thing she said to me was? Our mother. She stood in this cell. Where you are, she stood. And do you know what she said? 'Die like a Kelly, Ned.' A mother's last words to her son. But you, Dan. No, you want to get rid of that name. You want to scrape your family off your boot like shit.

DAN: I'm trying to stay alive, Ned.

NED: Can't say I like your chances. Staying alive was never your strong suit.

DAN: I just want to be forgotten.

NED: That's why you're staying away from them. Your own family. So you don't have to see the look on their faces as you turn your back on them.

DAN: You're not changing my mind on it.

NED: Am I not?

DAN: No, you're not. My mind's made up.

NED: It's all made up, is it?

DAN: Yes, it is.

NED: So, what did you come here for? A cuddle? A pat on the back so you can be on your merry way?

DAN: I was hoping…

NED: Hoping?

DAN: I was thinking… that you might… give it your blessing.

NED: I'm afraid you have to elaborate on that one.

DAN: It occupies my mind, Ned. What you must think of me. What I did to you that day.

NED: So it should, Dan. I hope it takes up a large portion of it.

DAN: And I'm sure it's caused you some amount of puzzlement.

NED: You tried to shoot me dead! Yes. It was puzzling.

DAN: Could you not yell please, Ned?

NED: Dan Kelly never hurt a single living soul. Oh. Except his brother, Ned, who he tried to shoot like a dog in the yard.

DAN: I was angry.

NED: Were you? I was lying on the ground, surrounded by coppers and bleeding my guts out. Thirty bullets in me and ninety pounds of armour on. Unless it was some unintelligent form of mercy-killing on your part? [*Beat.*] I thought not.

DAN: It'd gone wrong. Your plan.

NED: You could've shot at the coppers, Dan. Could've come to my rescue. But no. You shot at me. Tried to kill me. And here I am. Now I'm here.

    Beat.

DAN: I'm sorry I shot at you, Ned.

NED: Fuck off.

DAN: Not entirely sure I can, Ned. I tried. Got all the way to the border. The river at Wadonga. Started having these dreams.

NED: Dreams?

DAN: You stare at me in my sleep.

NED: I stare at you?

DAN: Your eyes. Just your eyes. I see nothing else. Staring at me. Every night. All night long. I wake up with the sweats. Screaming now and then. One time with a gun in my hand. Right there in my hand. That's a fire you can't run away from, I reckon. That's a fire that follows you. Until you put a gun in your mouth. Or a river in your lungs. Figured your blessing'll free me of it. Your forgiveness. Your word that we're all right, the two of us.

NED: And if I don't give it you?

DAN: It's nothing. A shake of the hand.

NED: Nothing?

DAN: I was dead to you a minute ago. I'll be dead to you again. All I'm asking is a fare-thee-well.

Beat.

NED: Have you ever saved anyone, Dan?

DAN: What?

NED: Have you ever saved anyone?

DAN: From what?

NED: Anything. A drowning. Have you ever saved anyone from a drowning?

DAN: You know I haven't.

NED: I have.

DAN: I know you have.

NED: And I know you do. But do you know what it's like?

DAN: Haven't you told us enough times what it's like, Ned?

NED: Not that part.

DAN: Haven't I held up your hero's sash for all to see a thousand times?

NED: Not that part! The other part. The part they don't warn you about before you run to someone's rescue. The part no one told me when I was a boy. Into the water I went and the Shelton boy was already under. I get to him and he looks at me. And is it surprise and gratitude in his eyes? Does hope spread across his wee little face? No. He panics further still. He grabs me, drags me under and holds me there as if I'm land itself. Nearly drowns me, he does. And he doesn't care. He's just trying to live. Half of me wants to be free of him and let the bugger drown. The other half makes me fight for him. And there we are in the water together, twisting and drowning each other. Because what they don't tell you is that it can get you killed, saving people. And it's the people themselves that are the greatest threat to you.

DAN: I'm not a threat to you, Ned. It's only gratitude you'll have from me.

NED: And it's permission to abandon our family you'll have from me. Do you think I'd do that after everything I've done? After what you did to me?

DAN *grips his bible.*

DAN: Maybe's there's something I can do for you, Ned. In exchange. Can't imagine it's going to be all that pleasant, what's to follow. You must be scared. Maybe I can help you in some way.

Beat.

NED: I hear you had quite the funeral.

DAN: Sorry?

NED: Three whole towns were ready to fight the coppers for your body. So they handed you over. You're in Greta cemetery, next to Steve. In consecrated ground. And Joe. He's in Benalla cemetery. Do you think I'll be put in consecrated ground, Dan? Think I'll get a funeral for my friends and family?

DAN: I'm sure they'll do the decent thing.

NED: The decent thing? [*Beat.*] Do you remember the likes of Mad Dan Morgan?

DAN: Yes.

NED: Do you remember playing make-believe when we were boys, pretending we were in his gang? Off to fight the coppers.

DAN: I remember.

NED: Brutal bastard he was and they shot him down for it. Afterwards, the coppers cut his head from his body to make a death mask. They ripped off his face as a souvenir. And proceeded to play football with his head. The coppers. A thousand pounds reward they put out for his capture. Eight times that we had on us. So what do you think they'll do to me?

DAN: I don't know.

NED: I keep looking at this part and that, wondering what they'll do to them. I want a proper burial, Dan. My body whole. In consecrated ground.

DAN: Well, I don't carry consecrated ground around with me, Ned.

NED: I'm sure the request of a priest would go a long way with the Gaol Governor. The others weren't that interested in helping.

DAN: I'm not a priest. I'm a wanted criminal.

NED: I'm sure he won't notice.

DAN: I'm not sitting down for a cup of tea with a man who wants me dead.

NED: He thinks you are dead.

DAN: And if he suddenly realises I'm not?

NED: I thought you had something to offer.

DAN: That's a fairly large something, Ned. [*Beat.*] Look. Maybe it won't even come to it. People are still trying to get you free. There's thousands in the city. All wanting you cleared.

NED: It won't matter.

DAN: Sixty thousand people put pen to paper, Ned. Fifteen hundred stood outside the Supreme Court and demanded a retrial. Coppers had to hold them back. There was a good old fight. You'll walk free of it, I reckon.

NED: Walk free?

DAN: Straight out the doors. Word'll spread across the whole country. The untouchable Ned Kelly.

NED: They turned down my last appeal. I hang tomorrow morning.

DAN: There's still—

NED: There isn't. They're going to hang my neck from a rope until I'm dead. If all goes well, my neck will break from the drop. Do you think it'll go well, Dan?

DAN: I don't know much about it.

NED: Maybe you will. Maybe you'll find out for yourself.

DAN: Are you going to turn me in, Ned?

NED: Should I not? You're a wanted criminal.

DAN: And your brother.

NED: Is that the rule, is it?

DAN: Look, Ned. It's an honourable thing wanting to save your soul…

> NED *laughs.*

NED: I don't want consecrated ground to save my soul. I want it because I deserve it.

DAN: Deserve it? Ned. You killed people.

NED: Yes, but they weren't very nice people.

DAN: There's nothing I can do, Ned.

NED: So you get a gravestone and I don't? Is that it? A man like you gets an entire town weeping in grief and a man like me gets ripped apart and shat upon for all eternity? Or do you require reminding of my many and varied feats and fucking accomplishments? Including many a personal debt unpaid to me by yourself.

DAN: I didn't come here for trouble.

NED: No. You came to ask a dead man for the right to live. That's trouble for one of us. [*Beat.*] What did you think, Dan? You'd just walk in here and we'd shake hands? Shed a few tears together and off you'd hop, up to your Queensland heaven?

DAN: I suppose I did. Yes.

NED: And why is that?

DAN: Well, I thought that…

NED: Thought what?

DAN: I thought that, in some manner of speaking, from a certain perspective, you owed it to me.

NED: I owe you? What do I owe you for, Dan?

DAN: Things.

NED: Things?

DAN: Things you did.

NED: What things?

DAN: Things in some of the situations we found ourselves in.

NED: I owe you for things I did in some of the situations we found ourselves in? That's very specific of you, Dan.

DAN: Actions you took.

NED: Which actions, Dan?

DAN: Actions that may not have been necessary.

NED: Fuck, Dan. Would you fucking say one?

DAN: Fitzpatrick. Fitzpatrick is one.

Beat.

NED: I think we may have differing recollections on that event.

DAN: I remember it just fine.

NED: Is that right?

DAN: Yes, that's right.

NED: Where were you sitting, Dan?

DAN: What?

NED: Where were you sitting? You were here, were you not? That's right. You were here and your sister Katie was here, on Constable Fitzpatrick's knee. He was holding pretty Katie on his lap, his hands all over her. She gave him a fight but he held on, didn't he? And you were just sitting here, watching. Do I have the basic proximities in order?

DAN: Yes.

NED: And it was you Fitzpatrick was here for. A warrant for horse thievery. That's right, isn't it Dan? But he'd taken a liking to Katie. Ma, she didn't like Fitzpatrick. So she hit him in the head with a shovel. And got herself thrown in gaol for it. But not you, Dan. You just sat there watching him hold your sister on his knee. She cried for you to help. I heard her as I got to the house. And in I came and saw what I saw. I drew my gun and fired to scare him off. And up he jumps and what does he shout? What does he shout, Dan?

DAN: That you shot him.

NED: As him. The copper.

DAN: What?

NED: Say it as him. Fitzpatrick. What did he say?

DAN: I'm not pretending I'm him.

NED: Come on. Make believe. What does he shout, Dan?

DAN: 'You shot me.'

NED: Nice and loud, Dan. Like him.

DAN: 'You shot me.'

NED: He yelled it, Dan!

DAN: 'He shot me! Ned Kelly shot me!'

NED: I didn't shoot you! Stop playing the fool! [*Prompting*] 'I've been shot...'

DAN: 'I've been shot!'

NED: 'By...'

DAN: 'I've been shot by Ned Kelly!'

> NED *grabs* DAN *roughly.*

NED: You do my family harm again you bastard and I'll blow your heart out your arsehole. Do we understand each other? And he said...

DAN: 'You're dead.'

NED: 'The lot of you...'

DAN: 'The lot of you. Every Kelly in the district. Dead.'

> NED *throws* DAN *aside.* DAN *falls to the floor, dropping the bible.*

NED: And then I threw him out the door.

DAN: The point of that was?

NED: To illustrate my act of heroism.

DAN: Well, you could've done it in the third-fucking-person.

Leon Cain as Dan and Steve Rooke as Ned in the 2012 Queensland Theatre Company production. (Photo: Rob MacColl.)

NED: Was it accurate?

DAN: Accurate enough.

NED: So tell me, Dan. Which part of that do I owe you for?

DAN: The part where you drew your gun. When a fist would've been enough. And not brought the whole of the Victorian Police after us.

NED: I was angry.

DAN: He was a copper.

NED: You let a drunkard's hand go up the skirt of your own sister. And in doing so you might as well've put a hand up there yourself. Might as well've been him. And now look at you. Can't even betray your family on your own. You need my permission to do so. If I told you to shove your cock up your own arse, I do believe you'd look behind yourself to see if there was a way.

DAN: I wouldn't look behind myself.

NED: I think you would look behind yourself.

DAN: Why would I look behind myself?

NED: Because try as I might, I can't recall a single moment of your entire life that you weren't a complete and utter invertebrate.

DAN: It wasn't him I was scared of, Ned. It was you. What I knew you'd do. What you'd bring down on top of us. I couldn't move I was so scared. And you did just what I knew you would.

> *They stare at each other.* NED *turns away. He picks up* DAN's *bible.* DAN *climbs to his feet nervously.*

Could I have that back please, Ned?

NED: Have what back?

DAN: That.

> DAN *grabs the bible.* NED *doesn't let go, staring at* DAN, *suspicious.*

NED: Getting a bit lost in the part, are we?

DAN: I want it back is all.

> NED *lets the bible go.* DAN *clutches it, moving away from* NED.

NED: You're very convincing in your little role there, Dan.

DAN: Thank you.

NED: Clutching your good book like your very soul depended on it. It makes me wonder.

DAN: What are you wondering, Ned?

NED: I'm wondering how far you're willing to take this.

DAN: What do you mean?

NED: To get what you came for. If you have anything more up your sleeve.

DAN: I'm not following you, Ned.

NED: Well. To be perfectly honest Dan, I'm wondering if you're hiding a gun in your bible.

DAN: A what?

NED: A gun. A small one. In your bible there.

DAN: Why would I have a gun?

NED: To shoot me with.

DAN: And why would I do that?

> NED *holds up his chains and injuries.*

NED: Because this time you can do it right.

DAN: You have quite an imagination, Ned.

NED: Would you care to prove otherwise?

DAN: You want to look in my bible?

NED: No. I want to look in your eyes while you tell me you don't have
   a gun in your bible.
DAN: And then you'll believe me?
NED: And then I'll know.

   NED *waits.*

   DAN *makes himself look into* NED*'s fierce eyes.*

DAN: There's no gun in my bible, Ned. [*Beat.*] Can I look away now?
NED: Is this what you see, Dan? When you sleep at night?
DAN: Yes. That's what I see.
NED: All night, every night?
DAN: Yes.
NED: And how does it feel now, Dan?
DAN: Can I look away please, Ned?

   Beat.

   NED *turns away from* DAN. DAN *tries to recover.*

   Stringybark Creek.
NED: I'm sorry?
DAN: Things you owe me for. Stringybark Creek.
NED: That's a curious choice, Dan.
DAN: You killed that copper. You put a death sentence on our heads.
NED: And whose fault was that?
DAN: Yours.
NED: Recall the day with accuracy, Dan.
DAN: I recall it just fine.
NED: I tried to get their guns off them without a fight. Do you remember?
DAN: I remember.
NED: And who was your man, Dan? Which one were you covering?
DAN: I don't recall.
NED: Well, let me remind you.

   NED *holds* DAN*'s hands as if pointing a rifle into the distance.*

   Him. That's yours.
DAN: Jesus, Ned.
NED: Keep your gun on him, Dan.
DAN: I'm not playing make believe like a child.

NED: We bail them up. Joe and Steve get their guns and we send the coppers back to town on foot. And then you said what?

DAN: I don't remember.

NED: You asked me to send Steve away. Come on. Ask me.

DAN: Ned, send Steve away.

NED: Why? [*Beat.*] 'There's no reason…'

DAN: There's no reason for him to be here. He just came to see me.

NED: Will you be all right, Steve? Steve's under the impression he'll be fine, Dan. Just keep your gun on your man and we'll do all right. And you said…

DAN: What if he goes for his gun?

NED: Then you fire a warning shot. And you said.

DAN: What if I hit him? I don't want to shoot a copper, Ned. I don't want to kill anyone.

NED: Look at their horses, Dan. What do you see?

DAN: I see a wall, Ned.

NED: On the horses, Dan! What do you see?!

DAN: Saddles. Guns. Bags.

NED: Body bags, Dan. Shotguns and body bags. That copper Fitzpatrick has the whole of Victoria thinking we tried to kill him. These men want us dead. Understand? I won't let them hurt you. [*To the imaginary Police*] All right, you bastards. This is a bail up.

NED *watches* DAN*'s man going for this gun.*

DAN. [*No response*] Dan!

NED *turns his gun towards the unseen Policeman and fires. A deafening gunshot rings out.*

Beat.

DAN: I don't mean this as an insult, Ned. But have you gone stark raving mad in here by any chance?

NED: He went for his gun and you were too scared to shoot. He pointed his gun at you and you still didn't shoot. And when it was over we had three coppers dead. And it didn't have to be a single one, if you'd been the least bit useful.

DAN: As a matter of fact, Ned, I was referring to the other one. The one you chased through the trees.

NED: He was dying. I put him out of his misery.

> KENNEDY *climbs out of the shadows, clutching his stomach.* NED *watches him.*

KENNEDY: I'm done, Ned.

DAN: You shot him.

NED: We had it out like men and he got the worst of it.

KENNEDY: End it for me, Ned.

NED: It was a mercy.

KENNEDY: End it quick.

> NED *buries his hand in* KENNEDY's *chest. A gunshot.* KENNEDY *dies.*

DAN: I was there, Ned. I followed you.

NED: I thought you had a bullet in you.

DAN: I saw how it went. What you did.

> KENNEDY *crawls away from* NED, *clutching his stomach.* NED *watches him.*

KENNEDY: Oh, Jesus. Oh, Jesus. Help me.

DAN: I saw how scared he was as he ran.

KENNEDY: He's going to kill me. Ned Kelly's going to kill me.

DAN: And how eager you were.

KENNEDY: Jesus or the fucking Devil, save me!

DAN: And you shot him and he dropped his gun.

KENNEDY: [*overlapping*] Please, Ned.

DAN: And you shot him again. But you weren't done even then.

KENNEDY: [*overlapping*] My family. Ned, my family.

DAN: And he was crawling and begging you for his life.

KENNEDY: [*overlapping*] I'm a father, Ned. I'm a father!

> DAN *points his hand towards* KENNEDY *like a gun. A gunshot.* KENNEDY *dies.*

> NED *stares at* KENNEDY, *confused.*

DAN: Ned? Are you listening to me?

NED: That's not what happened.

DAN: You killed him. And you didn't have to.

NED: There was no point to his suffering.

DAN: There was no mercy in your eyes, Ned.

NED: They shot you! They shot my baby brother! What should I have done?

> *Beat.*

> KENNEDY *stands, becoming the* GUARD. NED *and* DAN *look at him, surprised by his sudden presence.*

GUARD: What's all the yelling about?

DAN: We were just … disagreeing.

GUARD: About what?

DAN: A spiritual matter.

GUARD: Spiritual matter?

NED: Whether I'd rather see the face of the devil or stay here and have to keep looking at yours. I'm currently fifty-fifty.

> DAN *opens his bible.*

DAN: [*reading*] 'And Jesus said unto them "If you have no sword, sell your cloak and buy one". And they replied "Lord, we have two swords". And Jesus said "That is enough".'

GUARD: Well, I'm sure you'll change your mind when you get down there.

DAN: [*reading*] 'He went to the Garden of Gethsemane and his disciples followed him there.'

NED: Fifty-fifty's not bad. Considering.

DAN: [*reading*] 'And Judas, who was one of the twelve, appeared before them. And with him a detachment of soldiers and some officials from the chief priest and Pharisees.'

GUARD: Don't worry, Kelly. I'm sure your mates are down there waiting for you, quality human beings that they were. The glory of The Kelly Gang, hey? Rabid inbred dogs. Suppose we should thank you.

NED: For what?

GUARD: For getting them all killed.

> *The* GUARD *exits, laughing.* NED *is motionless, somewhat lost.*

NED: I'm of a mind to write to his superior. He's becoming downright irritable. [*Beat.*] It's a trap by the way.

DAN: What is?

NED: What your Jesus friend is doing. In your reading there. In his Garden. Grab a weapon. Lure them in. Make your stand.

DAN: He goes there to pray, Ned.

NED: Often pray with swords, does he? It's a fight he's after.

DAN: He gives himself up.

NED: Maybe he gets to it and changes his mind.

DAN: Should you really be blaspheming in your final hours?

NED: Should you really be impersonating a priest? [*Beat.*] How did Steve die? At Glenrowan. Leave him to burn did you?

DAN: He was already dead.

NED: Shot?

DAN: He drank the poison. What Joe gave us. If things went wrong.

NED: Did you talk him into it?

DAN: Why would I talk him into it?

NED: One body for the two of you. Only one of you can get away.

DAN: If I knew there was a body, I'd have sent Steve on his way.

NED: Would you?

DAN: He was my friend.

NED: Katie was your sister. You tried to kill me. God knows what end Steve Hart met with.

DAN: I saw a spare body the moment after Steve was still. It was too late.

NED: Best horse rider in the whole of Victoria. Handsome too. Like me and Joe. Although he did like to frock up in women's dresses an awful lot though.

DAN: It was you that told him to wear them.

NED: For reconnaissance. I didn't tell him to enjoy it. And you're the one who helped him in and out every time.

DAN: I knew how the laces went.

NED: Funny though. He never let me and Joe see him in a dress. Every time we had to send him out, off you'd both go into the bushes. Same when he came back.

DAN: He didn't want to be laughed at.

NED: Is that what it was? [*Beat.*] Was he angry with me? At the end?

DAN: We were all angry with you.

NED: Not Joe. Raised his glass. 'To the Kelly Gang'.

DAN: I thought he was taking the piss.

NED: He wasn't.

DAN: Are you sure about that?

NED: Joe was loyal. A perplexing concept to someone such as yourself.

DAN: You're right, Ned. Most loyal dog in existence had nothing on Joe Byrne. And didn't he love to make you happy? Didn't he walk on air whenever you gave him a 'job-well-done'? Writing your letters to the newspapers for you. And ballads for the masses to sing your praises. To raise your army. Ned's Irish Republic. The legend of Ned Kelly, born out of the pathetic adoration of a delusional obsessive opium-addict.

NED: Christ, you've been holding on to some things.

DAN: I've never seen a man so happy as Joe Byrne the day you made him Lieutenant of The Kelly Gang.

NED: Are you jealous, Dan?

DAN: It wasn't a real title, Ned. You made it up. Next to a shitter out the back of some pub.

NED: That he was my second and not yourself? That I trusted him more than you.

DAN: You weren't there, Ned.

NED: Where?

DAN: The night he killed Aaron.

NED: Aaron Sherritt was betraying us to the coppers.

DAN: So said the coppers.

NED: He said he wanted to shoot Joe Byrne and fuck his dead body before it was cold. That's an unusual thing to say, Dan.

DAN: The coppers said he said it. You weren't there. You didn't see the smile on Joe's face as he knocked on the door. Or the look of surprise on Aaron's when Joe Byrne blew a hole in his neck with a double-barrelled shotgun at point blank range.

NED: Joe was loyal to us. He was loyal to me.

DAN: They were mates, Aaron and Joe. Childhood friends. Why would Joe of all people believe a copper over his oldest friend? Has it not occurred to you, Ned? So he could prove to you how loyal he was. How much he cared. That he'd kill his dearest friend if you told him to. Aaron's innocence be damned. And wasn't Joe pleased as punch when you agreed to it? Weren't you both? Feeding off each other. Oh yes, Ned. Joe was very loyal.

Beat.

NED: I did like Young Steve quite a lot. And he never actually hurt anyone. Quite the innocent as it turned out. And you have to admit, he did look pretty in a dress.

DAN: How do you know that?

NED: Because I saw him, Dan.

DAN: He wouldn't let anyone see him.

NED: But he let you see him, didn't he?

DAN: Were you spying on us?

NED: Can't say that I was, Dan. But I certainly know how long it takes to get a woman's dress off. And you two, well, you two just took far too long. So I came looking for you. I'll admit, I'm ignorant in the finer points of getting out of a woman's dress. But it was your nudity I found confusing. There he was, leaning on the tree, skirt hoisted up and looking back at you. He was frowning at you as I recall. Sort of annoyed. And what was it he said to you? What was it he said?

DAN: 'Don't be a coward, Dan.'

NED: And full credit to you. Because in the moment that followed there wasn't a cowardly bone in sight. You did look quite happy afterwards, lying there together. Were you in love, Dan?

DAN: Don't be stupid.

NED: Just the cold was it?

DAN: We were just being boys is all.

NED: Funny. I don't recall me and Joe spooning in the bushes.

DAN: Well, at least we didn't get anyone killed. At least we didn't work each other up and rip a man apart like a pack of dogs. Like you and Joe.

NED: And it's comments like that which will never make you Lieutenant of The Kelly Gang.

DAN: Jesus.

NED: And if I recall correctly, you were more than happy to come along for the ride. Happy to hide behind me each and every step of the way, your total lack of contribution notwithstanding. Don't forget, Dan. I kept you alive. So you can go right ahead. You can bring up all the happy memories you please. I don't owe you a fucking thing.

Beat.

DAN: Will you be of assistance to them, Ned?

NED: What?

DAN: In the morning. At your hanging. Will you be of assistance to them?

NED: I intend to go quietly, if that's your meaning.

DAN: You'll put your hands behind your back when they want you to?

NED: I suppose I will.

DAN: You'll walk from here to there?

NED: That's right.

DAN: You'll climb the steps and stand under the cross beam when they ask you to?

NED: Yes.

DAN: And you'll let them cover your face? Put the rope around your neck? And you'll stand there, waiting for them to do their business?

NED: I'll be throwing some clever last words in there somewhere but that seems to be the order of events.

DAN: You won't fight them for your life?

NED: I've no fight left in me.

> DAN *offers* NED *his bible.*

DAN: But you have your own terms.

> NED *takes the bible, opens it and looks inside.*

NED: Not a gun then.

DAN: Not a gun.

> NED *takes a small vial from a hole cut into the pages.*

NED: Joe's poison.

DAN: From Glenrowan. 'One for each of us. If things go wrong.'

NED: You kept it?

DAN: I was half a day away before I realised it was still in my hand.

NED: Joe's poison. Got it from a Chinaman. What was it he said? If you take it and change your mind.

DAN: I believe it was 'Piss in your mouth'.

NED: Piss in your mouth. Could you imagine a more frustrating moment?

DAN: There's no pain in it, Ned. A pull in the stomach is all. No walk.

No rope.

NED: Is this the death of a Kelly?

DAN: A Kelly dies how he chooses.

NED: Maybe I choose the rope.

DAN: And if it doesn't go to plan? If you hang from too high or the rope is too hard? Your head can rip clean off you know? One moment you're screaming through your mouth and the next from your open neck. Is that how you want to go?

NED: Are you trying to alarm me with horror stories?

DAN: You're not scared?

Beat. NED *looks away.*

It's a new executioner you'll be having. Brand new. Nervous. Hands shaking. What if he gets it wrong, Ned? What if you're remembered for the most gruesome drop anyone ever laid eyes on?

NED: Then I'll stain their bloody floor from here to kingdom come.

DAN: Have you ever wondered why they do it, Ned? Why all the formality? Why the device? Why not throw you in the yard with a gun in your hand and ten armed men to shoot down? See how long you last.

NED: I like those odds a lot better.

DAN: Because it's not your life they claim, Ned. They can have that whenever they choose. It's your spirit they want. You walk to the rope and they have you. You agree with them by taking part in it. Give them your life if you've none left in you. But you can keep your spirit, Ned. Your pride can still be yours.

NED: Did you rehearse that?

DAN: Just the last part.

NED *stares at the vial.*

NED: Did he twist about?

DAN: Who?

NED: Steve. Did he twist about when he drank it?

DAN: I don't remember.

NED: If he twisted it was painful. Did he make any sounds or fall badly?

DAN: You want the details?

NED: If you're willing to educate me so thoroughly on one death you can do so with the other.

Beat.

DAN: He drank it. Then he lay back and shut his eyes. He never made a sound. Never said a word.

NED: Not too bad, all things considered.

DAN: So how about it, Ned? Escape their clutches one more time?

NED: Would they think well of me?

DAN: Who?

NED: Everyone.

DAN: A cheer would go up, it would. All across the city.

NED: So much for famous last words.

DAN: It'll be remembered better than any words, Ned. Better and longer I'm sure.

> NED *tries to open the vial. He struggles with both injured hands. He holds it out to* DAN.

NED: Can you help me with the lid? My hands are bloody useless.

> *Beat.*

DAN: It's just a blessing.

> NED *realises.*

NED: You're a bastard.

DAN: I'll be happy to help you, Ned.

NED: Is this a game to you?

DAN: I'll be glad to open it for you.

NED: It is, isn't it?

DAN: It's just your forgiveness, Ned. Nothing more.

NED: Did you make sure it was on good and tight before you came here?

DAN: Yes.

NED: And did you say all the correct things to me? Did you exploit my situation to your full satisfaction?

DAN: You'll have no walking to do. No hanging to do. Nothing I said was a lie. It's a fair exchange. A fare-thee-well. That's all.

> *Beat.*

NED: There's just one problem with your thinking, Dan. A minor detail that you've failed to realise.

DAN: What?

NED: I've got a bottle of claret coming my way.

DAN: What?

NED: My last meal. It's to be roast lamb, green peas and whole bottle of claret to myself. I haven't had so fine a feast in years. I'll not be missing that on account of your pissy little wishes.

NED *puts the vial back in the bible and gives it to* DAN.

DAN: You'd rather hang?

NED: Some meals are worth a hanging. I'm sorry you went to so much trouble. Fancy clothes and all.

Beat.

DAN: I didn't even know what size I was. At the maker's. He asked me and I couldn't answer. No idea what size of clothing I am. A grown man. I've been wearing your old clothes my whole life, I've never known a proper fit. Just the space I don't take up. [*Beat.*] Do you remember that fire when we were kids? Six or seven I was and Uncle Jim had come home drunk.

JIM *enters, drunk.*

JIM: [*singing*] 'In the sweet by and by, we shall meet on that beautiful shore. In the sweet by and by, we shall meet on that beautiful shore.'

DAN: And he kept howling for something I can't recall.

JIM: Come on, Ellen. Give us a go, love. I'll pay you fair and all.

NED: He wanted to fuck our grieving widow of a mother for a shilling.

JIM: Out by the pigs. No one need know of it.

DAN: Is that what it was?

JIM: He's dead, Ellen. Me big brother is dead. The father of your kiddies. Always thought he was a someone, he did. But he's just a Kelly like the rest of us. And now he's even less.

DAN: And a fight broke out.

NED *confronts* JIM.

JIM: I can be their Daddy, Ellen. Boys need a father. Or they go rabid. Like dogs!

NED *hits* JIM *in the stomach, sending* JIM *to the ground.*

DAN: And then he threw something at the house.

NED: He threw a lamp.

A smash. A fire.

DAN: And set the house on fire. With Mother and me and the girls inside it.

JIM: Jesus. Jesus.

JIM exits.

DAN: And there was smoke everywhere and people grabbing each other and pulling. And before I knew it I was alone. I didn't know what to do. Where to go. And Ma and the girls were screaming for me. Over and over. I remember those flames, flicking at me. And then you charged in, tall and strong. Broke the door clean off its hinges. And I swear the flames themselves shook at the sight of you. And you threw me over your shoulder and you said 'All right now'. That's what you said. 'All right now.' And out we went. I could have been resting in a tree you stood so strong.

The fire and memories fade.

What'll it take, Ned? What'll it take for you to help me? To get what I came for?

NED: Do you think I'd make it?

DAN: Make what?

NED: If I got out the door? Got to the street?

DAN: What do you mean?

NED: Do you think I'd have support? Get out of Melbourne?

DAN: If you got to a crowd maybe.

NED: Are there a lot of them out there?

DAN: Thousands. Coppers couldn't get within a street of you.

NED: It's not that far you know. From here to the street.

DAN: Are you kidding, Ned?

NED: It's not impossible.

DAN: It's highly fucking unlikely.

NED: Die like a Kelly, she said.

DAN: I think she was talking more along the lines of tuck in your shirt and stand up straight.

NED: So imagine what she'll think of this.

DAN: You're serious, aren't you?

NED: Has anyone ever done such a thing?

DAN: No. They haven't, Ned. And you know why? Common sense.

NED: Don't kid yourself. It's not that common.

DAN: Right. Okay. And assuming you're ready to die in a hail of gunfire.

NED: Which I am.

DAN: Which you are. How exactly do you plan on getting through the whopping great big door?

NED: With your help.

DAN: Come again?

NED: That unattractive guard that comes in and out. He won't be expecting a priest to jump on his back now, will he?

DAN: And I'll be living up to his expectations and all. They'll catch me, Ned. Shoot me down or string me up beside you.

NED: Or we'll get away. The Last Ride of the Kelly Gang. It'll be all they talk about for years to come.

DAN: I don't think you're thinking straight, Ned. If at all.

NED: This is how you get remembered, Dan.

DAN: I don't want to be remembered. I want to be forgotten. I want to forget all of it.

NED: Brave old Dan. Braver than Ned himself.

DAN: I didn't come here for trouble. I came here to talk and that's all.

NED: And to poison me.

DAN: To help you pass quietly.

NED: I don't want to pass quietly. I want to pass noisy as hell.

DAN: What about your lamb and your peas?

NED: I'd rather eat dirt as a free man.

DAN: You'll be a dead man. And lambless and pealess to go with it.

NED: You want my forgiveness? This is your chance.

DAN: Ned. Stop.

NED: Here's the plan.

DAN: Oh, Jesus.

NED: You get him to the ground and we march him out with your poison in his jaw. First bugger to try anything, the poison goes down his throat.

DAN: They'll kill us, Ned. All three of us.

NED: It'll be quick if it happens. Are you with me, Dan?

DAN: Please don't.

NED: I'll take that as a yes. [*Banging*] Oi! Where are you, you ugly bugger? I'm in need of judicial assistance!

DAN: Jesus. Jesus, Ned.

NED: Watch your language, Father.

DAN: You've killed me. You've fucking killed me.

NED: On the contrary, I'm about to make you a legend.

> The GUARD *enters.*

GUARD: Well?

NED: Well what? Oh, right. Well, we were having somewhat of a disagreement and we were wondering if you'd be so kind as to resolve it for us.

GUARD: I don't have time for games, Kelly.

NED: Come on now. There's no harm in it. I'll be out of your hair first thing tomorrow.

GUARD: What's it about then?

NED: My brother. Dan Kelly.

GUARD: What about him?

NED: We were disagreeing on his present whereabouts.

GUARD: His whereabouts?

NED: His location. Where he is, as it were.

GUARD: Last I heard, he's six feet under in Greta.

NED: And you're sure of that, are you?

GUARD: Where else would he be?

NED: Maybe you should ask the Father.

> The GUARD *looks at* DAN. DAN *manages a confused shake of the head.*

Well, he says that Dan Kelly is on his way up to heaven. But I say he isn't. I say he's burning in hell. So where do you think he is?

GUARD: Jesus, Kelly. I don't know, you mad bastard.

NED: No, think on it now. Pretend you're intelligent. The Father, he's of the mind that Dan Kelly was harmless. A perfectly nice person who deserves his freedom and sunshiny reward. Now, I happen know for a fact that Dan Kelly is spineless and a traitor and deserves to reside nowhere but the lowest level of Hell. So the way I look at it, the deciding factor is you.

GUARD: Why me?

NED: On account of your general thickness. A layman's view of things. So. Where do you think my brother is? [*Beat.*] Any time now.

GUARD: He's where every last one of you Kellys is headed. Up Satan's arsehole.

> The GUARD *rams his truncheon into* NED*'s stomach, sending* NED *to the ground.*

Well, what do you know? I didn't do too badly after all.

> The GUARD *puts his truncheon to* NED*'s throat.*

You make things worse and I'll make things worse. Up and up we'll go until one of those times, I'll come in here with a gun.

NED: Not even this?

GUARD: What?

NED: You'll even let this pass, will you?

GUARD: What the fuck are you talking about? Irish bloody lunatic.

> The GUARD *exits.*

DAN: I'm sorry. I couldn't. I couldn't do it.

NED: You know what, Dan? You don't deserve the name Kelly. You don't deserve your sister's tears and you don't deserve the right to die beside me. You deserve your gutless paradise and may you live forever in it.

DAN: Are you forgiving me, Ned?

NED: And here I was looking forward to that roast lamb all week long. Do you want your forgiveness, Dan?

DAN: Yes.

NED: Then I'll give it you. If you'll do me one small favour.

DAN: What favour is that?

NED: Show me that you're a man.

DAN: What?

NED: At Glenrowan, when I came back to save you. Show me it wasn't a waste, what I did. Show me I didn't kiss my mother goodbye for nothing.

DAN: What is it you're asking me to do?

NED: I'm asking you to kill me, Dan.

DAN: What?

NED: With your poison. Here and now. Before they do it.

Hugh Parker as the Guard and Steven Rooke as Ned Kelly in the 2012 Queensland Theatre Company production. (Photo: Rob MacColl.)

DAN: I'm not going to kill you, Ned.

NED: Finish what you started. Put me out of my misery. Like I did for that copper.

DAN: This is ridiculous.

NED: You think I want to hang for trying to save something like you? A pathetic little weakling.

DAN: You're not thinking straight, Ned.

NED: You want your freedom without guilt on your back? You want warm Queensland sunshine? You want a long and happy life knowing your brother's at peace with you?

DAN: I'm not going to kill you, Ned.

NED: Well, that's a right shame. You'll excuse me for killing you then.

>   NED *gets his chain around* DAN'*s neck, choking him.*

Come on, you little pisser.

>   DAN *grabs* NED'*s hand and squeezes.* NED *growls in pain.*

That's it. Come on.

>   DAN *elbows* NED *and gets his head free of the chain.* DAN *punches him in the torso.*

That's not where they shot me, Dan.

>   DAN *punches again.*

Oh, come on. They shot me lots of places. You can find one.

>   DAN *brings his knee into the back of* NED'*s thigh.* NED *grunts in pain.*

That's the spot.

>   DAN *kicks* NED *and then again.* NED *laughs.* DAN *takes the poison from the bible and takes off the lid. He holds the poison up to* NED'*s mouth, staring at him.*

Don't be coward, Dan. Finish me off. [*Beat.*] I order you to do it! I order you to do it, Dan!

>   DAN *starts to cry.*

Quit your crying. Finish it.

>   DAN *pulls away from* NED, *crying.* NED *is left with the open vial in his hand.*

Beat.

You didn't kill me, Dan.

DAN: I'm sorry.

Beat.

NED: He wanted to kill you, you know? Joe Byrne. After you got those coppers killed at Stringybark Creek. I could see it in his eyes. He wanted you dead for what you'd done to us. For the death warrant you'd brought down on his head with your uselessness. We slept out that night. Word wouldn't get back until the next day. Our last night before the whole country would be after us. I didn't sleep. I just sat there. Watching Joe and waiting. He sat himself up, holding one of the copper's guns in his hand. And he came eye to eye with me. We stared at each other. And I held out my hand and he gave me the gun. And he lay back down and went to sleep. We never spoke of it, he and I. But I stopped him killing you that night. I think I'm stopping the whole world trying to kill you. And to tell you the truth, Dan, I give up. [*Beat.*] Drink it.

DAN: What?

NED: Your poison. Drink it.

DAN: Are you serious?

NED: I am.

DAN: It's poison.

NED: I know it's poison.

DAN: Why the hell would I drink poison?

NED: Because you're useless is why. Because you're going to die one day, Dan. Whether you like it or not. And when you do the guilt you carry for what you did to me is going to weigh you all the way down to hell. Drink that and I'll forgive you. It'll show me how much it means to you. You can die a guiltless death and your Jesus friend and all his bunny rabbits can give you cuddles in heaven.

DAN: I don't want to die, Ned.

NED: You'd be dead a hundred times over if it wasn't for me. You won't last a day when I'm gone. Might as well get it over with now. While you're warm and dry. Go on, Dan. Just a pull of the stomach, you said. No pain at all.

Beat.

DAN: I lied.

NED: What?

DAN: About the poison. It hurts.

NED: You said it didn't.

DAN: I know I did.

NED: You said Steve had a fine old time.

DAN: He was in pain. Worst pain I ever saw.

NED: But you were all right for me to be drinking it.

DAN: I lied to you. And I owe you an apology for it.

NED: Well. We'll just put it with the other ones shall we?

> NED *grabs* DAN *and shoves the vial into* DAN*'s mouth. He holds* DAN*'s mouth closed.* DAN *swallows and falls to the floor. He convulses and screams through his clenched jaw, in great pain.*

Ah, Christ. Are you going to scream all the way through it?

> *Darkness.*

> *Then…*

> DAN *wakes on* NED*'s bed.* NED *is sitting on the floor reading* DAN*'s bible.*

NED: Good morning.

DAN: Morning?

NED: You've been out all night. I told them you were keeping vigil and fell asleep. They'll be collecting me shortly.

DAN: They believed you?

NED: You were snoring.

DAN: What happened?

NED: What usually happens under such circumstances. I saved your gloomy little life.

DAN: How?

NED: I pissed in your mouth.

DAN: You what?

NED: I opened your mouth and pissed in it. You swallowed my piss and threw the poison back up again.

DAN: You pissed in my mouth?

NED: And healed you from on high with my excrement. Are you not going to thank me?

DAN: No, Ned. I don't believe I am.

NED: Why ever not?

DAN: You tried to kill me.

NED: You tried to kill me first. At least I bothered saving you. [*Indicating the bible*] This is bullshit. Dies for your sins and then comes back to life. What kind of sacrifice is that? If I could come back from the dead wouldn't I die for every sorry bastard on the planet as well?

> NED *throws the bible aside.*

DAN: What made you change your mind?

NED: I decided to test a theory for myself.

DAN: A theory?

NED: How long you can stay out for before it's too late.

DAN: That's it? And if I died with a mouth full of piss?

NED: They can't hang me twice.

DAN: I meant me, Ned. Did you not care about that?

NED: Can't say I did. Goodbye, Dan.

DAN: What?

NED: Go away. I no longer wish to proceed.

DAN: Why?

NED: Perhaps I'm afraid of what I might find out. About you and Steve.

DAN: You know all there is.

NED: Be on your way. Or I'll let the Gaol Governor know who you are. And they'll put you in the ground good and proper.

> *Beat.*

DAN: All right, Ned. You win. I'll get you your burial.

NED: Come again?

DAN: I'll talk to your Gaol Governor. Offer to take your body off his hands. Probably scared of an uprising as it is. Sure he wants to wash his hands of you. Wants you out of here as soon as possible.

NED: You're lying.

DAN: I'll take you home to the family. You can even have your choice of where you're buried. With Joe. Or me and Steve.

NED: Joe.

DAN: All right then.

NED: And all you want is forgiveness?

DAN: No. No, I want you to prove you're a good man first.

NED: What?

DAN: I want you to prove your forgiveness is worth a damn.

NED: Did you hit your head while you were lying there not moving?

DAN: You want your hero's funeral? This is how you're going to get it.

NED: Do you not think I'm a good man, Dan? Is it the coppers you side with now?

DAN: I don't know what I think anymore, Ned.

NED: You seem to be forgetting, Dan. They pushed me. I might have stolen a horse or two in my time but they treated me like an animal. Hunted me and pushed me as far as a man can be pushed. So I pushed back, good and fucking proper. And not a single civilian I hurt.

DAN: I recall a few civilians dying at Glenrowan.

NED: So we've come to it, have we?

DAN: I suppose we have.

NED: Well, for the record, Dan, I didn't kill anyone at Glenrowan.

DAN: No. But they died all the same.

NED: The coppers did the killing.

DAN: You put them in harm's way, Ned. Wasn't that your great plan? Take hostages. Draw in the coppers. Blow 'em away and start a war. All day long, you filled that inn with people. Knowing you wouldn't do them a lick of harm but the coppers would.

NED: Am I required to apologise for the victims of the Victorian Police?

DAN: You're a lightning rod, Ned. And the storm was coming. You didn't fire the bullets. The bullets were on their way and you put us all in front of them, in your stupid bulletproof armour. 'Fire away,' you yelled and they obliged you. Over thirty coppers, guns blazing. But the hostages behind us weren't bulletproof, Ned. Jack Jones who was thirteen and sang you a song on the piano and died screaming in pain wasn't bulletproof. His sister, Jane. George Metcalf. Martin Cherry. The rest who got bullets in them.

NED: I tried to get them out.

DAN: And why couldn't you?

NED: The coppers kept thinking they were with us.

DAN: And didn't you give them every reason to. You and Joe. In every word you said and letter you wrote. The great Ned Kelly, proclaiming the whole country belonged to you. Were you there, Ned? When the Reardon family got cut to shreds?

Sergeant STEELE *approaches out of the shadows.*

A mother and father and their children, trying to escape.

STEELE: Don't move.

DAN *picks up the pillow from* NED*'s bed and shoves it in* NED*'s arms.*

DAN: Margaret Reardon, with a baby in her arms.

STEELE: Hands in the air!

DAN: Screaming 'We're hostages'.

STEELE: Hands or I fire!

DAN: 'We're hostages!'

STEELE *fires.*

And the father scrambled for his children.

STEELE *fires again.*

And the copper hit their son.

STEELE *fires again.*

And he took aim at the mother and the baby in her arms.

STEELE *fires again, a deafening shot ringing out. The pillow is hit.*

STEELE *exits.* NED *stares at the pillow, shaken.*

There were other ways but you wanted a storm. A good old fight with all the bodies you could point at. To start your war. Ned's army. Ned's great republic. You might as well've pulled the trigger yourself. You might as well've been one of them.

NED: It was coppers like that I was fighting. Coppers who turn up with a warrant and take a liking to your sister. Coppers who turn up to arrest you with body bags. Coppers who kill a man when all he wants is what's fair.

DAN: When did we become soldiers, Ned? When did we go from running for our lives to fighting a war? It was you and the coppers. Egging each other on. Making things worse. They argue, you draw a fist. So they draw a gun. So you start a war. Up and up. All the while telling me to stay by your side where it's safe. All the while, making things worse and worse. [*Beat.*] Didn't Martin Cherry come into the inn as a lark? Not even taken prisoner. Just walked on in to meet you. Didn't he shake your hand and smile like you were the whole world to him? And didn't you love it? 'I'm Kelly's prisoner,' he kept giggling and had a good old time. Until he got a bullet to the groin. He wasn't smiling when he died, Ned. And neither was Joe. And neither was Steve. And don't say the guilt of their deaths isn't inside you because I know it is. And I have the proof of it.

NED: You have proof of it, do you?

DAN: I do. Your supporters, Ned. Over a hundred supporters you had, lying in wait nearby. Your secret army, ready and waiting in the dark for your signal to attack from behind. To light the spark. Start your revolution. You only had to give the word and they'd have rushed to our rescue. They were ready weren't they, Ned?

NED: They were ready.

DAN: To charge the police lines.

NED: It would have been a war and no less than a war.

DAN: And you got to the trees. You got to them, didn't you? During the fight.

NED: Yes.

DAN: So why didn't they charge? Why didn't they, Ned?

NED: Because I changed my mind.

DAN: Why?

NED: Because I didn't want anyone else getting killed. [*Beat.*] They weren't an army. They were old men, women and children. Starving Irish farmers. Some didn't even have a gun. A shovel or a stick was all they had. They would have been massacred. So I sent them home. You should've seen the look on their faces.

DAN: So you spared them the fate you brought to others. Because you'd seen the horror of it. Because you felt the guilt of it.

NED: I suppose that's accurate enough.

DAN: And you damned the rest of us straight to hell.

NED: I came back to save you.

DAN: You failed.

NED: Do you have no knowledge of what I did that day? What I did for you? What the whole fucking country is still talking about?

DAN: I have my view of it.

NED: Then you'll have mine. I could have gone too, Dan. I could have got away and disappeared forever. But I looked back at the inn. That little house, surrounded by coppers. I thought of your stupid face, smiling. 'Of course he's coming for me', you'd be thinking. No question in your mind. Two dozen bullets in me, half my blood gone and ninety pounds of armour on. I could barely stand let alone walk. But off I went, closing in behind them. To save my baby brother. The first one sees me lurching out of the mist. They hadn't got a proper look at me in the dark. And here I was, this thing coming at them. Steam from the helmet, sunrise in their eyes. 'A headless monster', he screams. And didn't I look the part. He fires his gun, hits me, but I stay on my feet. Others see me, scared out of their wits. They had no idea what the fuck I was. They fire their guns and I fire back. One empties his gun at me and it doesn't slow me down one bit. Another shoots me in the face, breaking my nose against the helmet. And I congratulate him on it. 'It's the devil', they scream. And for a moment I wonder if they're right. They fire rifles and shotguns but I push forward. Half the bullets going in but I'm too far gone to stop. More dead than alive, I was. I yell at you to come out and fight. Surely you will. I keep looking at the door, screaming your name. Smashing my gun against my helmet again and again, ringing it like a bell. Waiting for you to charge. But there's no sign of you. The coppers are on all sides of me now but I'm not stopping until I get to you. I'm not stopping. And then the strangest thing happens. Joe's horse comes up to save me. She just wanders up to me, ready to ride and take me away from it all. As if the ghost of Joe himself is on her, telling me to leave you there. But I don't. They shoot her twice and she falls. And then a bullet rips through my hand and I know this is it. This is my death. I scream at you to get out and I push forward, shooting at anyone I can, wanting every bullet in the place to head my way so you can get clear. And one of them gets in close behind me with a shotgun and takes me out at the knees. They rip the guns from my hands and the helmet from my head. And they realise who they've been fighting. I lie there pinned to the ground while the Victorian Police argue over whether to shoot me dead on the spot. One of them points his own gun at the other coppers and threatens to kill anyone who does me harm. At that point I was fairly certain I'd seen it all. And then you proved me wrong. I was the first to see you. Coming out the front door of the inn. No helmet on. Your rifle in your hands and the devil in your eye. I'd never seen such a look on your face. 'Jesus', I thought. 'The brave bastard is trying to rescue me.' And then you start shooting. But not at the coppers. No. At me. Screaming your lungs out. Firing again and again. The coppers have to drag me away to protect me from you. After everything I'd just done. A coward your whole life and it's me you try to kill.

DAN: Over a hundred people you were supposed to come back with. An army. That's what you promised us. Not you, staggering around like a drunk. I watched you fighting them. I kept looking into the mist, waiting for a charge of people. And then I saw you fall and I knew. You'd got into your head you could do the whole thing yourself. It was like something exploded inside me. I've never been so angry. I pushed Steve out of the way and ran out the door. And Jesus, Mary and Joseph I wanted to put a bullet through your head. And I would've. I would've got you. But I got hit in the leg, ran back in and I just stood there, looking at all the bodies, all your wreckage. The legacy of the great Ned Kelly. Dead civilians, dead friends and dead children.

NED: You looked at all the bodies, did you?

DAN: That's right.

NED: So you lied to me.

DAN: What?

NED: You told me you only saw a body for your miraculous escape after Steve's body was still. I let your body go still, Dan. I waited a considerable portion of time before I pissed in your mouth. There was ample opportunity for you to save your friend. So I'll ask the question again. And I assure you it will be for the final fucking time. How did Steve die?

  Beat.

DAN: I killed him.

NED: Why?

DAN: We had a fight. Not even a fight. It was... The coppers had lit the fire. And you weren't coming this time. And I got the idea.

There'd be smoke and we could escape through it. Steve was upset. Thought we'd get shot if we tried. He didn't want to bother any more. Wanted it all over with. He was holding his poison in his hand and I was holding his hand and trying to tell him things to stop him. I told him we'd get away. That we'd head to Queensland and forget everything. Change our names. We could live together and be happy. Be together. And in love. And he looked at me like I was thick. And he said. 'Don't be stupid, Dan. We were just being boys is all.' Like it didn't mean anything to him at all. And I looked at the poison in his hand. And his hand in my hand. And I shoved it into his mouth. And I held his mouth shut and he swallowed. His eyes went wide and his jaw locked. He screamed through his teeth. And he shook. And he died. [*Beat.*] Am I brave now? Am I a Kelly now, Ned?

Beat.

DAN *cries.*

NED *turns away, heartbroken.*

Beat.

NED: What was it he sang? The Jones boy, on the piano. Just before the coppers showed. What was it he sang for me?

DAN: 'Wild Colonial Boy'.

NED: What are the words?

DAN: I don't remember.

NED: I've heard you sing it often enough.

DAN: 'There was a Wild Colonial Boy,
            Jack Doolan was his name,
            Of poor but honest parents,
            He was born in Castlemaine.
            He was his father's only hope.
            His mother's pride and joy,
            And dearly did his parents love
            The Wild Colonial Boy.'

NED: And then he just skipped to the last part. The Jones boy. What was the last part?

DAN: 'He fired at trooper Kelly,
         And brought him to the ground,
         And in return from Davis,
         Received a mortal wound,
         All shattered through the jaws he lay,
         still firing at Fitzroy,
         And that's the way they captured him,
         The Wild Colonial Boy.'

NED: Isn't that strange?

DAN: That they rhyme ground with wound?

NED: That he just went from the first verse to the last. As if what got Jack Doolan there didn't matter. As if there aren't a thousand choices you make. I should've… [*Beat.*] I'm no good, Dan. At the end of the day, I think I'm just no damn good. I wish you'd finished me that day. You deserve it more than them.

DAN: I would've if I could shoot worth a damn.

> *They laugh gently.*

NED: You have my forgiveness, Dan. And my apology. Live a long life. Free of the likes of me.

> *Beat.*

> DAN *spits in* NED's *face and throws him to the ground.* NED *is shocked.*

DAN: Fuck your forgiveness.

NED: What?

DAN: I said fuck your forgiveness. And fuck your regret.

NED: But it's what you wanted.

DAN: Yes. It was. And then you poisoned me and pissed in my mouth. I can't say I find myself in need of forgiveness from someone such as yourself.

NED: My burial.

DAN: What about it?

NED: You promised.

DAN: You're not going in consecrated ground, Ned. You know why? You're too famous. They want to remember you, Ned. They don't ever want to forget you. They're going to cut off your head as a souvenir. They're going to tear you open. They're going to dig their hands into you and rip out every organ they can reach. And they're going to stuff them into jars for their cabinets and conversations. And when they're done ripping you to pieces, when they've had their fill, they'll dump whatever's left in a hole in the yard and leave it to rot.

NED: They won't touch me. I'm Ned Kelly. I'm a national fucking hero.

DAN: They're killing you, Ned. They don't want you part of their country.

NED: I Am This Fucking Country!

Beat.

DAN: No, you're not. Me, maybe. But not you. You're just a glorified horse thief. The wrong man pushed too far and nothing more. Goodbye, Ned.

DAN *goes to leave.*

NED: Maybe you're right, Dan. But do you know what you are?

DAN: What? What am I?

NED: Alone. You're alone, Dan. No friends. No family. So afraid of dying, you can't even bear to live. They won't even know your name. I die today. But I'll be alive when it happens. And they'll be getting my name fucking right.

DAN *is motionless.*

The GUARD *enters.*

GUARD: It's time, Ned.

NED *goes to* DAN *and kisses him on the cheek.* DAN *doesn't look at him.*

NED: Enjoy the sunshine. You deserve it.

NED *leaves.*

The GUARD *turns to* DAN.

GUARD: Awake now, are we? [*No response.*] You have to go now, Father.

DAN: I'm Dan Kelly.

GUARD: What?

DAN: I'm Dan Kelly.

GUARD: I don't understand.

DAN: My name is Dan Kelly.

GUARD: Dan Kelly's dead, Father.

DAN: He's not dead.

GUARD: Look, I'm not in the mood for games.

DAN: He's standing in front of you.

GUARD: They saw him die. It was in all the papers. He's got a grave and everything.

DAN: No. Listen to me.

GUARD: Come on, you nutter. Out.

DAN: I'm alive. I'm standing here. My name is Dan Kelly.

GUARD: And I don't appreciate being made fun of. There's a lot of important people here today. I'll give you a minute to pull yourself together and then you're out. [*Leaving*] Mad fucking Irish.

   The GUARD *exits.* DAN *yells at him.*

DAN: I'm Dan Kelly! I'm Dan Kelly! I'm Dan Kelly! [*Beat.*] ...I'm Dan Kelly.

THE END

www.currency.com.au

Visit Currency Press' website now to:

- Buy your books online
- Browse through our full list of titles, from plays to screenplays, books on theatre, film and music, and more
- Choose a play for your school or amateur performance group by cast size and gender
- Obtain information about performance rights
- Find out about theatre productions and other performing arts news across Australia
- For students, read our study guides
- For teachers, access syllabus and other relevant information
- Sign up for our email newsletter

The performing arts publisher

www.ingramcontent.com/pod-product-compliance
Lightning Source LLC
Chambersburg PA
CBHW041935090426

42744CB00017B/2062

* 9 7 8 0 8 6 8 1 9 9 8 7 0 *